PASTELS ARE GREAT!

John Hawkinson

Albert Whitman & Company — Chicago

Other Art Books by
John Hawkinson
COLLECT, PRINT AND PAINT FROM NATURE
MORE TO COLLECT AND PAINT FROM NATURE
OUR WONDERFUL WAYSIDE

BEFORE YOU BEGIN...

In this book about pastels there are many things to do. Maybe you'll find too much for you or maybe not enough. But I hope that this book will not be just something for you to look at or copy. I hope that it will inspire you to learn to use pastels. As you get ready, here are some ideas to help you.

Have fun practicing the different strokes by making designs with them. If you have a difficult time mastering one or two of the strokes, don't worry or fret. Just think up some strokes of your own to take their place.

Be sure to work large so that you don't fall into the trap of using your fingers. That can spoil everything.

If you finish something you particularly like but there are a few smudges, tap them with a kneaded eraser. It will pick up some of the color. If you must rub a pastel drawing, do it with a paper napkin instead of your fingers.

I have nothing against the traditional method of using pastels— I call it the futsy-putsy method—except that it's too messy for children and it's not much fun to do.

Anyone who teaches or writes how-to books on art hopes, of course, that the student will become an ardent observer of everything around him. This, as we know, is what really makes an artist. Since no one I've met has much success in making a child observe either by trick or threat or other devious means (such as a school assignment), I am going to be direct. Please go out and look at the world. There is so much to see, so much to share through art!

John Hawkinson

Pastel is the name for a kind of art and for the tool the artist uses. Pastel is color in its purest form, ground and pressed into sticks. If you use this art tool well, there are many surprising things to do with it.

Pastels are made in many grades, shapes, and sizes. Some have oil added to prevent smearing. Some pastels come with paper wrapped around each stick. Peel it off, or you will have to use your pastels like crayons. I think the square shape is best to work with, but you may like the round or hexagon shape better.

Pastel drawings can be sprayed with a fixative to keep them from smearing. But someone who is just learning to use pastels does not need to do this. A great help in learning art is a large waste basket.

Here are the eight pastel strokes that you will learn in this book.
Each new stroke lets you draw more things you see or imagine.

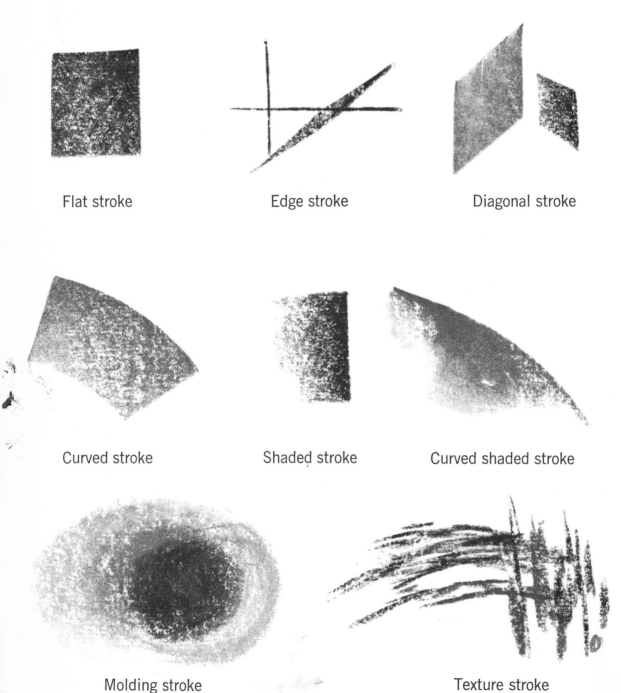

Flat stroke   Edge stroke   Diagonal stroke

Curved stroke   Shaded stroke   Curved shaded stroke

Molding stroke   Texture stroke

Values

Each of these strokes can have many values, or shades. The harder you press down on your pastel, the darker the value becomes. Less pressure gives you a lighter value.

Values can be built up by making one stroke over another—one, two, three, or four times, like this.

These different values can be used to make planes or surfaces that float in space. They can be put together to make a solid object, such as a block or house.

7

There are cool colors, warm colors, bright colors, soft colors, and dark colors.

There are so many colors that it's hard to know where and when to use them.

It's good to start slowly. Just use three colors for a design or drawing. But never stop experimenting. Try light pastels on dark paper, then dark pastels on light paper.

8

Each color has many values, from light to dark. By experimenting, find the colors that make the most values. Blue, for example, will give you more values than yellow.

What happens when you put one pastel stroke over another — yellow over blue? See how many greens can be made by using different values of the same blue and yellow. Try this with other colors.

There are many ways to experiment with color. Here are just a few.

Getting Ready

You will hold the pastel in the same way for all the strokes in this book. Before you begin, break each stick into three pieces of different lengths. (Of course there are other ways to hold and use the pastel. Later you can find interesting ways of your own.)

Almost any kind of paper will do. Newsprint and construction paper are cheap and good. In any case, the surface under the paper will determine the texture of the pastel. If you experiment with and without padding, you will see the difference. A section of newspaper does very nicely, or several sheets of the paper you are using will do. As you work, put your finished papers under the pile.

So here we go — not to paint a picture but to experiment with this special color tool. We won't be copying watercolor or oil-painting methods. We won't use pastels like crayons. We're going to draw with pastel, a wonderful, exciting medium.

You need a chair or stool and a table that's not too high so that you can sit as shown here.

Have ready your box of peeled and broken pastels. (If they are oil pastels, put a layer of cotton in the box to keep the sticks from touching each other. They pick up color from each other very easily.)

Put your paper and padding in front of you. Place your free hand on the edge of the paper, as you see here.

The Flat Stroke

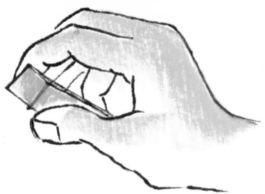

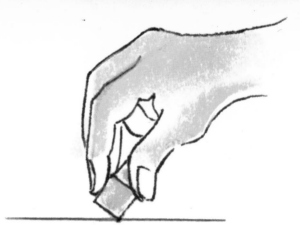

Now pick up a piece of pastel and hold it in your fingers, like this.

Place the pastel on the paper, like this.

Hold your arm parallel and above the paper. Then your arm will not brush across and smear the pastel. You will use your arm, not your fingers, to make all the strokes in this book.

Draw the pastel down. It should make a square or rectangle, like this.

Try this flat stroke again, but with less pressure and then more pressure. Fill at least six sheets of paper with shades of pastel color in long and short strokes. Next, try overlaying colors to make patterns. Find out what happens when you blend certain colors.

The Edge Stroke

Hold the pastel in the same way, but move your hand sideways, like this. You can make a thin line that is very straight. In fact, it may look as if you used a ruler.

You can make vertical lines by turning the paper halfway around or moving your arm.

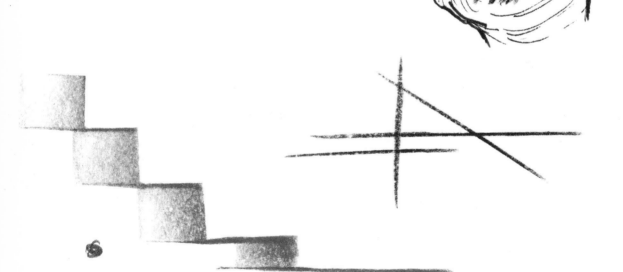

If you have trouble making this thin line, try making stairs going up and down.

By using flat and edge strokes together you can make abstract designs, tall buildings, and anything else rectangular.

The Diagonal Stroke

The diagonal stroke looks simple, but some-times needs practice. Turn the pastel in your hand so that it rests on the paper at an angle, like this.

It should look like this...

...but if it looks like this, it's not right. It's just a square drawn at an angle.

Try making a square first and then make the diagonal stroke on the side and bottom. Now you have a box or cube.

The diagonal stroke is a wonderful one for designs — putting roofs
on little houses, making battleships, and giving buildings a real look.
Try at least a sheet of different kinds of designs, abstract or geometric.
Remember to shade by pressure of the hand.

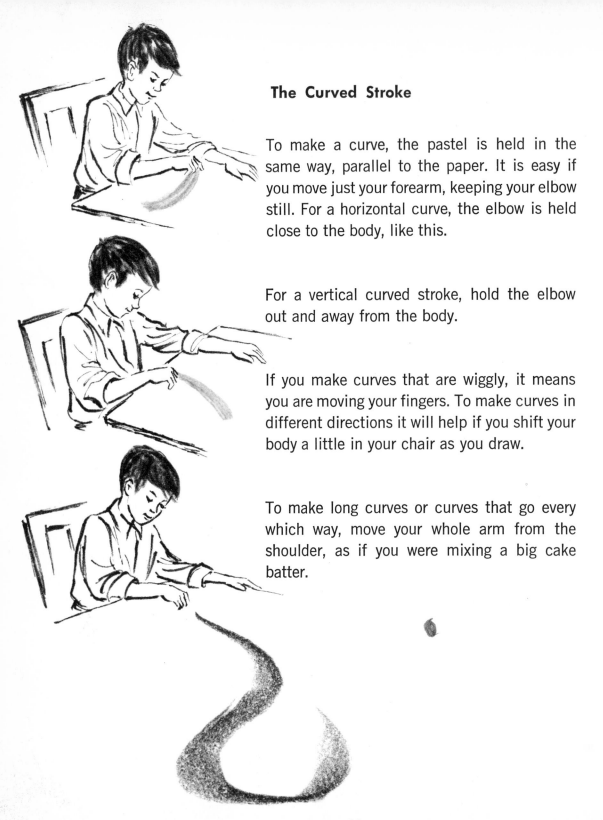

The Curved Stroke

To make a curve, the pastel is held in the same way, parallel to the paper. It is easy if you move just your forearm, keeping your elbow still. For a horizontal curve, the elbow is held close to the body, like this.

For a vertical curved stroke, hold the elbow out and away from the body.

If you make curves that are wiggly, it means you are moving your fingers. To make curves in different directions it will help if you shift your body a little in your chair as you draw.

To make long curves or curves that go every which way, move your whole arm from the shoulder, as if you were mixing a big cake batter.

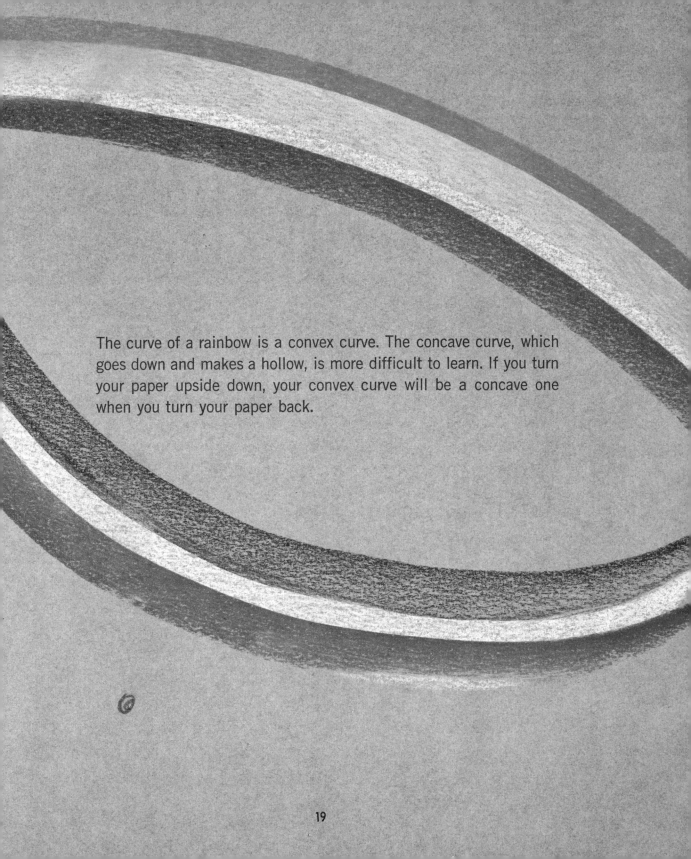

The curve of a rainbow is a convex curve. The concave curve, which goes down and makes a hollow, is more difficult to learn. If you turn your paper upside down, your convex curve will be a concave one when you turn your paper back.

Lettering

Because nearly every artist is asked to make signs, try lettering with pastels. Hold the pastel firm and never move your fingers. Turn the paper, turn your body, move your arm, but don't move your fingers.

These letters are easy, straight down and straight over. Use flat and edge strokes.

For these letters, turn the paper, turn your body, arm, or hand, but don't move your fingers. Hold the pastel firm. Use flat, edge, and diagonal strokes.

BCDGJ
RSUOP

These letters use all the strokes you have learned: flat, edge, diagonal, and curved. The curved strokes are made by moving your arm only. Try printing your name as a start.

ROBERT

Your letters should look something like this.

ROBERTA

If your letters look something like this, you are moving your hand or your fingers.

By combining the curved strokes with straight or diagonal strokes you can experiment with drawing many new things, real and abstract.

You can draw real and imaginary animals and many designs. Details can be added with a felt-tipped pen or ball-point.

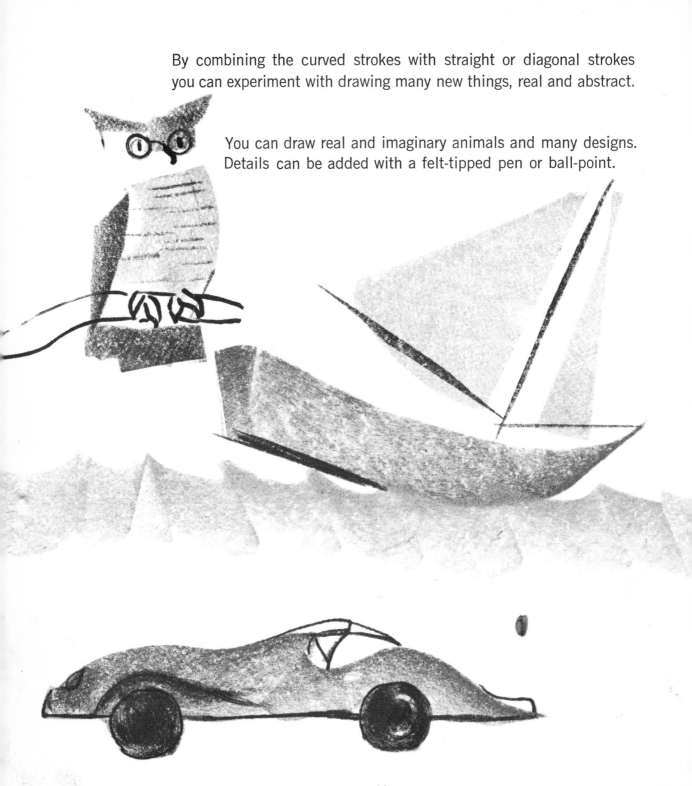

People doing things are fun to draw with pastels. You and a friend can take turns drawing and posing for each other. Use hands, feet, and every part of your body when you pose. A few seconds are long enough.

Use the strokes you have just been learning. You'll make lots of mistakes — throw them all away. When you run out of paper, get yesterday's newspaper and use that.

If you can't find a partner, follow your mother around the house while she's working and draw her. Watch your little brother or sister at play.

If you don't like people, try monsters with green faces and happy smiles — and of course use the strokes you have learned this far.

Most of us can see horses on TV, in movies, or maybe in our own backyards, and most children love horses. Try drawing them with pastels. Begin by getting some photographs of horses — it would be better still if you could bring a horse into the house for a model.

On these drawings, the arrows show the direction of the stroke and the twist. Use hand and arm, but not fingers. Hold the pastel as you have been doing for all the strokes.

Of course all curved strokes don't have to be so controlled as those in drawings of objects. Free-form curves like ribbons can flow in all directions and colors from your hand. By moving your wrist as well as your arm, you can change the direction of the curve.

Turn music on, the kind you like, and draw with the rhythm and tune. You'll find if you sit straight in your chair you can follow the music with your body from the hips up. Choose your pastels at random, close your eyes, listen, and let go. You'll probably be pleased and surprised when you see what you've drawn.

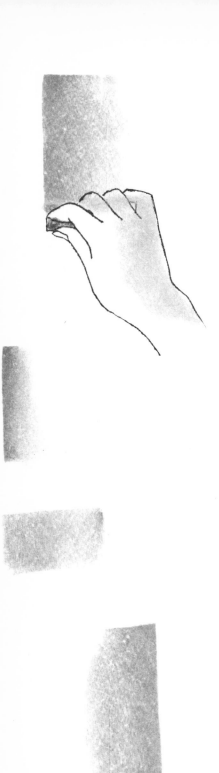

The Straight Shaded Stroke

Until now you have done all the shading of color by pressing the pastel flat on the paper. Here is a new stroke that is shaded from dark to light.

Hold the pastel as you have been, flat to the paper. Press down firmly on one end of the pastel, but let the rest touch the paper ever so lightly. Draw the pastel down and see what you get. Your stroke should have a hard, dark edge and fade gradually to nothing.

If your stroke looks like this, you are not holding the pastel flat enough.

If it looks like this, you are holding the pastel too flat.

If you are right-handed and want to make a stroke like this, press the opposite end of the pastel down, tilting it a little as you do so.

Try varying the width of your shaded stroke by changing the angle of the pastel and your hand. This will let you control the width of the stroke, as here.

With this shaded stroke you will be able to make curved or cylindrical objects like rockets, tree trunks, ash cans, and stovepipe hats, as well as more kinds of abstract designs.

The Curved Shaded Stroke

The curved shaded stroke is an easy step from the straight shaded stroke. It adds a tremendous number of new things you can do.

Here are just a few things you can draw with this stroke. How many more can you think of?

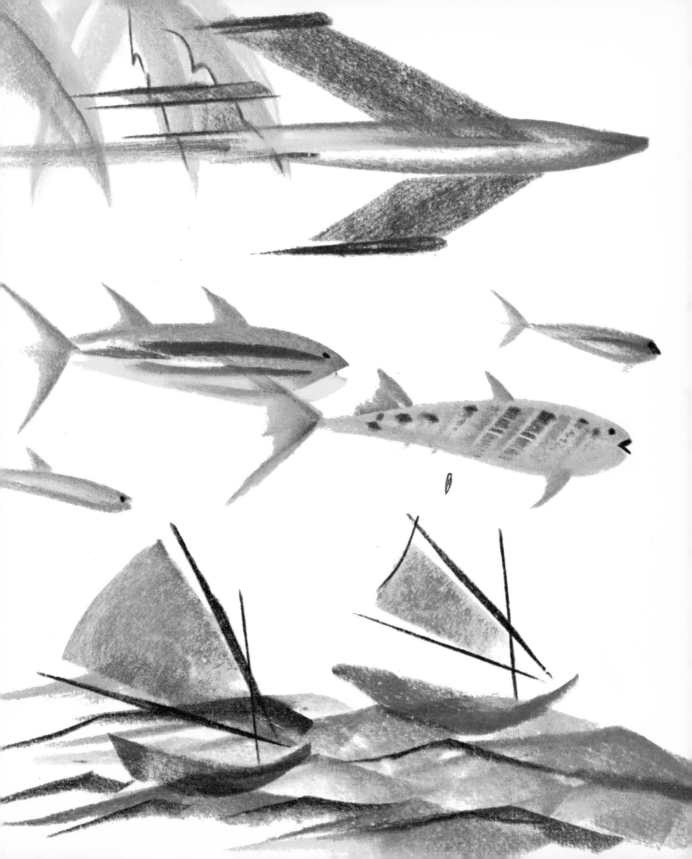

For a streamlined object, like an airplane or fish, the top or convex curve is fairly easy. All you have to do is make a graceful arc as you put more pressure on the end of the pastel.

To make the bottom, or concave, stroke is more difficult. Press on the heel of the pastel and move your arm as if you were following the movement of a clock pendulum. If this seems too hard, just turn the paper upside down and repeat the top stroke. For vertical objects, such as vases or rockets, turn the paper or move your elbow away from your body. See if you can draw a horse, using curved shaded strokes.

The Molding Stroke

The next stroke, the molding stroke, is simple to do. Hold the pastel flat down on the paper and move your arm in a circular motion, like this.

Start at the center of whatever object you want to make and gradually work out. Shading can be done by going over the center area two or three times. This may make a loose powder on the surface of the paper. Blow this off before going on — although this can be a wonderful way to mix colors, it is messy.

Use molding strokes for a scene — the sun shining brightly, a tree
and bush full of leaves, perhaps a horse dashing past.

When you want to draw people you can begin with a molding stroke. Try drawing a friend while he or she draws you. Sit up straight and use your eyes to look down. In this way you can be an artist and a model at the same time, or you can take turns. Try to draw life-sized, it's easier.

Start by molding the head and neck, as in Step 1. For the hair, use a flat curved or molding stroke, Step 2.

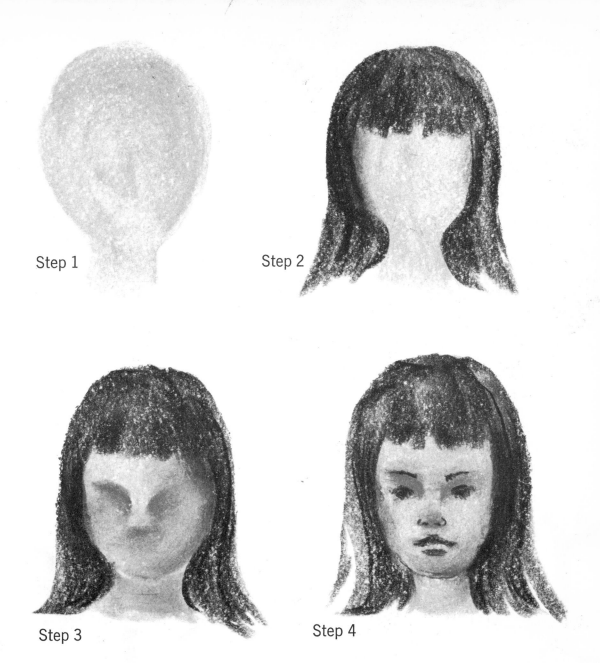

Step 1

Step 2

Step 3

Step 4

Add shape to the face. You can use flat or shaded strokes to make the eye socket, cheek, and chin, as in Step 3. Color is not nearly as important as shape. Last, Step 4, add the details of the eyes and mouth.

If there are pets such as dogs, cats, turtles, or fish in your house, use them for models.

We have a cat named Sam. He sleeps a lot and makes a good model. We got him when he was a kitten.

We used to have a dog named Flash, and before that, a dog named Sandy. Flash was smooth. Sandy was shaggy.

We've had big turtles and small turtles, but all of them had shells with thirteen sections.

We've had goldfish, too,

... and a parakeet who flew around the house and said, "Look out! I'm an eagle!"

The Texture Stroke

The texture stroke is easy. Hold the pastel as you have been doing and move your hand rapidly back and forth. Use this stroke mostly for tree foliage. Here you see it used with shades of gray, but mix colors freely when you use the texture stroke.

43

Whether you live
in a big city,

or a small town,

high on a mountain,

or on a farm,

... you will be able to draw the world you live in with pastels.